# CHANGE

Written by

**EMILIE DUFRESNE**

Designed by

**DANIELLE RIPPENGILL**

**RESPECT TRANS PEOPLE**

# BookLife
## PUBLISHING

## Image Credits

**POWER TO THE PEOPLE**

**EQUAL RIGHTS**

**BE YOURSELF**

**BLACK LIVES MATTER**

**SOME PEOPLE ARE GAY GET OVER IT!**

# CONTENTS

Words that look like this are explained in the glossary on page 30.

# HAVING PRIDE

## What Does It Mean to Have Pride?

Being proud of who a person is or something they have achieved is a feeling that someone can have. A person might also be proud of themselves for who they are or the things they have done.

## What Is Pride?

As well as being a feeling or emotion, Pride is the name given to an event that happens in many places around the world. The event often includes a march and celebration for the LGBTQIA+ community. Pride is a time for people in the LGBTQIA+ community to celebrate and take pride in who they are. It is also a time for people to talk about what still needs to be done for the LGBTQIA+ community.

SPREAD L♥VE NOT HATE

# What Does LGBTQIA+ Mean?

The letters that make up LGBTQIA+ mean many different things about sex, sexuality and gender identity.

## Sex

A person's sex is to do with their **biology**. It can refer to the **biological sex** they were **assigned** at birth, or it could be the sex they identify with.

## Sexuality

Sexuality is a way of talking about a person's sexual identity. This is to do with the ways in which a person may or may not feel **attracted** to people, and what people they are attracted to.

## Gender Identity

Gender identity is a person's idea of how they are **masculine**, **feminine**, a mixture of both of these, or neither of them.

# A Closer Look at the Letters

There are lots of different combinations and versions of the LGBTQIA+ letters that people might use. As people learn more and more about sex, sexuality and gender, lots more letters and meanings can be added.

**Bisexual**
This is a person who is attracted to more than one gender.

**Transgender**
This is when a person's gender identity is different to the biological sex they were assigned at birth.

**Gay**
This can be men or women who are only attracted to people who are the same sex as them.

**Lesbian**
This is a woman who is only attracted to other women.

The LGBTQIA+ community is often **represented** by a rainbow flag. This is because it shows how everyone is different and unique and that it is these differences that are beautiful. Let's take a look at some LGBTQIA+ people who can take pride in the way they have changed and are still changing the world!

### Queer
Someone might see themselves as queer if they feel their sexual and gender identities are anything other than **heterosexual** or **cisgender**.

### Intersex
This is a person who is born with a mixture of **sex characteristics** that are seen as male and female, such as **genitals** and **chromosomes**.

### Asexual
This is a person who does not feel sexually attracted to any sex or gender.

### Plus
This is used to include all the letters that are missing from the abbreviation and to make sure everyone in the LGBTQIA+ community feels included regardless of who they are. This can include people who are **pansexual** or **gender fluid**.

# BAYARD RUSTIN

Born: 1912 Died: 1987

## Fighting for Civil Rights

Bayard Rustin was an American activist in the civil rights movement. He spoke out against how Black people were being treated in the US at the time. Bayard was good friends with Martin Luther King Jr, and together they organised many marches. Bayard believed in protesting without being violent or causing damage. The marches and events that Bayard organised were very important in bringing Black people together to protest during this time.

FIGHT BACK!

BLACK LIVES MATTER

## Out and Proud

Bayard was an openly gay man throughout his life. During this time, it was not safe to be openly gay in the US and many people treated the LGBTQIA+ community badly, so the work Bayard did for the civil rights movement often wasn't celebrated in public. However, many people now look back and see Bayard as one of the most important civil rights and gay rights activists of the time. This is because he was open about his sexuality in a time when it could be dangerous to do so.

The real <u>radical</u> is that person who has a vision of <u>equality</u> and is willing to do those things that will bring reality closer to that vision.

## The Civil Rights Movement

The civil rights movement happened in the US during the 1950s and 1960s. During this time, many Black people were campaigning for equal rights. Unfortunately, many Black people in the US were experiencing <u>discrimination</u>, <u>prejudice</u> and violence. The movement achieved a lot, and laws were created to protect the lives of Black people and bring them closer to equality. However, there is still more that needs to be done to protect the Black community across the world.

EQUAL RIGHTS

# BARBARA JORDAN

## Born: 1936 Died: 1996

### Making History

Barbara Jordan grew up in the south of the US. From a young age, she found that she was very good at speaking publicly. She studied law at university but quickly became involved in politics. In 1966, she became the first woman to be elected to the Texas Senate. In 1972, she was elected to the US House of Representatives.

### Choosing Not to Come Out

After Barbara's death in 1996, it was revealed in her obituary that she had been in a relationship with a woman, Nancy Earle, for a long time. Barbara did not choose to come out publicly in her lifetime and that is okay; we can still look back and be proud of her achievements as a Black, gay woman during this time.

# What Is Coming Out?

Coming out is when a person chooses to tell someone about their sex, sexuality or gender identity. It is important to remember that a person doesn't have to come out unless they want to or are ready to. A person also doesn't have to come out to everyone they know at once – they can come out to whoever they want, whenever they want. The choice is theirs.

One thing is clear to me: we, as human beings, must be willing to accept people who are different from ourselves.

# IAN MCKELLEN

Born: 1939

> You just simply have to, one by one, change people's minds, and that can be done.

## Taking to the Stage

Ian McKellen has been interested in the performing arts since he was very young. He acted in many theatre productions and was most well-known for acting in plays written by Shakespeare. Ian has also acted in many famous films and is celebrated for his roles in *The Lord of the Rings* and *X-Men*. In 1991, Ian was <u>knighted</u> for what he has done for the performing arts.

## Speaking Up and Coming Out

Ian had known for many years that he was gay but had decided to only come out to his friends and family. Until 1967 in the UK, it was illegal for men to have relationships with other men, and even after this Ian worried that if he came out, people would not want to include him in their plays and films. However, in 1988, Ian decided to publicly come out as a gay man to openly stand against a new law that was made in the UK called section 28. Ever since, he has been an activist for the LGBTQIA+ community. As well as supporting many other charities, Ian was one of the <u>founders</u> of the charity Stonewall, a charity that aims to fight inequality and <u>empower</u> the LGBTQIA+ community.

## What Was Section 28?

Section 28 was a law that was brought in by the UK government in 1988. The law said that same-sex relationships could not be 'promoted'. Part of this law meant that gay relationships couldn't be taught or even talked about in school. Many LGBTQIA+ activists protested this law, but it was not <u>repealed</u> in the whole of the UK until 2003.

SOME PEOPLE ARE GAY. GET OVER IT!

# MARSHA P JOHNSON

**Born: 1945 Died: 1992**

## Finding Her Place

Marsha P Johnson was assigned male at birth. However, during her childhood she often chose to dress in clothes that were thought of as female. After finishing school, Marsha chose to leave her hometown and move to New York. It was here that she found more members of the LGBTQIA+ community and more transgender people like herself. Here she was able to be more open about her gender expression and she lived as a woman and changed her name to Marsha.

As long as gay people don't have their rights all across America, there's no reason for celebration.

## Starting the Stonewall Riots

In New York at this time, the LGBTQIA+ community were often targeted by the police. The Stonewall <u>riots</u> began as a reaction to the police <u>raiding</u> LGBTQIA+ clubs such as the Stonewall Inn and arresting many members of the community. The six days of rioting are thought to be the start of the gay rights movement that eventually spread throughout the US.

## A STAR of Her Own

After the Stonewall riots, Marsha founded the STAR organisation with Sylvia Rivera. STAR was a group that focused on helping young transgender people who were homeless in New York. It provided these people with <u>shelters</u> and <u>services</u> to help them have a better start in life.

**POWER TO THE PEOPLE**

# BOBBIE LEA BENNETT

### Born: 1947 Died: 2019

## Creating Change

Bobbie Lea Bennett was assigned male at birth, but after knowing that she was a woman for many years, she chose to have gender reassignment surgery. Bobbie was told that the money for her surgery would be given to her, but the payment was suddenly removed without explanation. To protest this, Bobbie drove across the country to wait at the offices of the people who refused her the money. She refused to leave until they would meet with her, and within three days she had received the money she needed to pay for her surgery.

## Representing Marginalised People

Being both a disabled person and member of the LGBTQIA+ community, Bobbie represents many different groups of marginalised people. Throughout her life, she fought for the rights of both disabled people and transgender people. She founded organisations and hosted talk shows which aimed to raise awareness about accessibility for disabled people.

## What Is Transitioning?

A transgender person may or may not choose to transition. Transitioning means a different thing to every person. It might involve medical transitioning, such as taking medication or having surgery. For someone else, it could involve telling friends and family, dressing differently and changing their name to one they feel suits them more.

# SYLVIA RIVERA

**Born: 1951 Died: 2002**

RESPECT TRANS PEOPLE

> I did a lot of marches. I had to do something back then to show the world that there was a changing world.

## Fighting from the Start

Sylvia was a transgender activist from New York. She was friends with Marsha P Johnson and they both fought for the rights of the LGBTQIA+ community in New York at the time. Sylvia had always fought for what she believed in. Being a young Latina transgender woman who was living in poverty, she understood the struggles that many marginalised groups faced.

# Doing It for the Community

Sylvia was involved in the Stonewall riots and fought alongside other members of the community for equal rights. The gay rights bill became law in New York in 1986. This was a law that made sure the gay community could not be discriminated against on the basis of their sexuality. However, the law did not protect the rights of the transgender community. Sylvia felt let down because the law didn't acknowledge or understand the struggles of many other marginalised groups within the LGBTQIA+ community.

## Coming Together as a Community

During Sylvia's lifetime, many members of the LGBTQIA+ community did not support each other in their fight for equality. It is important to remember that different people within the LGBTQIA+ community might be struggling for different reasons. For Sylvia, it was important that she still fought for the equality of marginalised groups in the LGBTQIA+ community after the gay rights bill was passed.

I got involved with a lot of the different things because I had to. I had so much anger.

# LAVERNE COX

**Born: 1972**

> We are not what other people say we are. We are who we know ourselves to be, and we are what we love.

## Being Seen in the Arts

Laverne knew from a young age that her gender identity did not match the male one she was assigned at birth. It was not until she was at university studying performing arts that she began to transition. She became an actor and started performing in many transgender roles. In 2014, she became the first transgender person to be nominated for an Emmy. Since her acting career began, she has been breaking down barriers for transgender people and taking on roles that made transgender lives and stories more represented and visible on TV.

We are born as who we are, the gender thing is something that is <u>imposed</u> on you.

## Spreading the 'T' Word

Through her fame, Laverne has also found a <u>platform</u> from which she chooses to speak out for LGBTQIA+ rights. As a transgender person of colour, she knows the struggles that many marginalised people in the LGBTQIA+ community face. She is not afraid to talk about and raise awareness of these issues and stand up for marginalised members of her community.

## What Are Representation and Visibility?

Representation is when lots of different people and their views are shown in something. It is important to make sure people of different <u>cultures</u>, sexes, ages, abilities and genders are all represented. Visibility is how well a particular group can be seen in a society. For example, Pride is an important event because it gives the LGBTQIA+ community visibility. Within Pride events, lots of different members from the LGBTQIA+ community should be represented.

**LGBT EQUALITY**

# ARSHAM PARSI

Born: 1981

## Living in Exile

Arsham was born in Iran. In 2004, he started his work in activism for LGBTQIA+ people in Iran by founding online groups for them. In Iran, being gay is against the law. This meant that in 2005, Arsham had to escape to Turkey. In Turkey, he continued his activism and worked to raise awareness of the struggles that LGBTQIA+ Iranian people were facing. Arsham was eventually given asylum in Canada. In Canada, Arsham was able to talk more publicly about his sexuality and the work he was doing for other LGBTQIA+ people in Iran and the surrounding countries.

> I have to change people's minds. I have to educate them that diversity and people's sexual orientation should be respected.

## Clearing a Path

His work continued and Arsham went on to make films about his activism. He also went on to be the founder of the International Railroad for Queer Refugees. This is a charity that aims to find homes for members of the LGBTQIA+ community who have fled from countries where it is dangerous for people to be open about their sexuality or sexual identity. Arsham's work with this charity has helped thousands of people in the LGBTQIA+ community.

## Fighting the Law

Although many places have laws that protect the rights of the LGBTQIA+ community, sadly there are still many places where this isn't the case. Luckily, there are many organisations and charities around the world that are working to make sure the LGBTQIA+ community is protected. However, lots still needs to be done to make sure people are protectedby the law everywhere.

# JONATHAN VAN NESS

**Born: 1987**

> What if everything I've ever been through was preparing me for this moment — to be strong enough to share this, and to share it on my own terms.

## Learning About His Gender

Jonathan always knew that he had a feminine side as well as a masculine side to his gender identity. He often liked to dress up in clothes that are thought to be feminine. This continued into his adult life, and after hearing about what it meant to be non-binary and gender fluid, Jonathan realised that these words helped him to express his gender identity. After soaring to fame after appearing on the TV show *Queer Eye*, he has felt able to use his platform to talk about his gender identity and show that a person's gender expression does not have to be either masculine or feminine but can change and move between the two.

I wanted to do something to move the conversation forward in a meaningful way around HIV ... and what it is to live with HIV, and to <u>humanise</u> and <u>normalise</u> a lot of the things I talk about.

## Having Hard Conversations

Jonathan also uses his platform to talk about how he is living with HIV. He hopes that by talking about the disease, it will show people that it is still possible to live a happy and healthy life. He also hopes that by being open about it, it will encourage others to do the same and raise awareness about how the illness is tested and treated.

## What Is HIV?

HIV is an illness that makes it hard for a person's body to fight off other infections that they might get. Currently there is no cure for HIV, but with the right medication it can be controlled.

# KIAN TORTORELLO-ALLEN

**Kian**
(He/They)

**Born: 2001**

> I am a ... <u>revolutionary</u> because I will change the world.

## Teenager, Transgender, Trendsetter

During his time at high school, Kian decided to come out as a gay transgender male. Kian found school a hard place after coming out and was bullied for a time. However, he felt that he needed to stand up for what he believed in. He worked to make sure that his school became a more accepting place for transgender people of colour.

BE YOURSELF

# Being the Change

Kian took his activism one step further by joining organisations such as the Gender Sexuality Race Alliance and by becoming a young leader for the Gay Lesbian and Straight Education Network. This meant that he could represent young, transgender people of colour in these organisations and make sure their struggles were heard. Kian could also make sure that people were doing something about these issues and that people were still fighting to improve the lives of transgender people.

# Making Your Own Platforms

Kian also uses social media to create his own platforms to communicate with his community and discuss important LGBTQIA+ issues. He helped to start the Instagram page @justlgbtstuff which aims to support LGBTQIA+ people of colour. Kian hopes to start his own organisation one day, but in the meantime he is happy to support others and keep being the change he wants to see in the world.

I realised that I had my own voice and I can also make my own platforms and I may be 17 but that doesn't mean that I don't have something to say and that I can't have my voice be heard.

# BE AN ALLY!

Being an ally for the LGBTQIA+ community is when a person who isn't LGBTQIA+ supports and stands up for other members in the community. Here is how you can be an ally that creates change for LGBTQIA+ people.

## Create Safe Spaces

Sometimes school can seem like a scary place for people. Why not create a club where everyone feels safe to express themselves? This could be an art club, a sports club or even an activism club. Whatever it is, try to make it a very accepting and inclusive space so that everyone feels welcome.

## Be the Change

A great way to start creating change is by being the change. By including lots of different people and treating people equally, it will influence other people to do the same.

## Celebrate Difference

Make sure that you celebrate difference in anything you do. If it is a play, a sports game or a project, try and make sure to include lots of different people.

# MORE MOVERS AND CHANGERS

There are so many LGBTQIA+ people who have created change in the world, let's take a look at a few more of them.

## Harvey Milk
Harvey was the first openly gay man elected as <u>governor</u> in the history of California.

## Simon Nkoli
Simon Nkoli was a Black rights and LGBTQIA+ rights activist in South Africa. He was open about having HIV in a time when people often didn't speak about it.

## Edith Windsor
Edith Windsor was an activist who fought to have same-sex marriage made legal in the US.

## Christine Jorgensen
Christine Jorgensen was one of the first people to discuss her transition in public in the hope that this would help other transgender people.

# GLOSSARY

| | |
|---|---|
| **accessibility** | how easy it is for someone to do or achieve something |
| activist | a person who tries to make a change in the world by doing things such as going to marches |
| **assigned** | to be given without having a choice |
| asylum | safety in another country from your own |
| **attracted** | to want to form a close, romantic or sexual relationship with someone |
| biological sex | whether a person's sex characteristics are considered to be male, female or intersex |
| **biology** | the science that studies the growth and life processes of living things |
| chromosomes | tiny things inside cells (the building blocks that make up all living things) that give our bodies information about what to do and how to grow |
| **cisgender** | when a person's gender identity matches the biological sex they were assigned at birth |
| community | a group of people who are connected by something |
| **cultures** | the traditions, ideas and ways of life of different groups of people |
| discrimination | the unfair treatment of people based on illogical reasons, such as their gender, sex, age, where they are from or what they look like |
| **elected** | being chosen to do something, often by a group of people |
| Emmy | an award that recognises excellence in the writing and making of television shows |
| **empower** | to give people the power to achieve certain things on their own |
| equality | the state of being equal, having the same opportunities and rights as someone else |
| **feminine** | things that are stereotypically associated with being female |
| founders | people who have set something up |
| **gender expression** | the ways in which people choose to express their gender |
| gender fluid | when a person's gender can switch between masculine or feminine or be a mixture of both |
| **genitals** | parts of the body between the legs |
| governor | a person who has been elected to help run a town or area |
| **heterosexual** | only being attracted to people of the opposite sex to you |
| House of Representatives | a part of the US government that manages the laws of the country |

| | |
|---|---|
| **humanise** | to make something more relatable to people and their emotions by making it clear how humans are involved and affected |
| imposed | forced upon, or given without agreeing to it |
| **knighted** | to have been given a knighthood by a king or queen for your achievements or services to a country |
| Latina | a woman or girl who is from Latin America or has family from there |
| **march** | a large gathering of people who walk from one point to another in order to try to change or celebrate something |
| marginalised | to have been treated differently because you are on the edge of a group or different to the majority of people in a particular place or community |
| **masculine** | things that are stereotypically associated with being male |
| normalise | to make something accepted and normal |
| **obituary** | a public announcement of someone's death |
| pansexual | when a person can be attracted to anyone regardless of their biological sex, sexuality, gender or gender identity |
| **platform** | the position a person holds that they can use to help make other people's voices and opinions heard |
| poverty | not having enough money to pay for important things |
| **prejudice** | opinions, judgements or beliefs that are formed without taking the facts into account |
| protesting | showing a disagreement to something |
| **radical** | a person who wants to do things in a completely new way that has never been done before |
| raiding | when the police break into a place without the people inside knowing, in an attempt to arrest people |
| **raise awareness** | to try to make sure lots of people know a lot about a certain thing |
| repealed | to have removed or taken away |
| **represented** | acted as a symbol for something else |
| revolutionary | a person who does something in a new way that has never been done before |
| **riots** | acts of public disturbance that are often violent and include lots of people |
| Senate | a very important part of the US government |
| **services** | things that are there to help people with things such as health care and housing |
| sex characteristics | behaviours or physical features that tell you of a person's biological sex |
| **shelters** | places for people without a home to stay for a short while |

# INDEX